# BUILT TO LAST?

The Buildings of the Northamptonshire Boot and Shoe Industry

Published by English Heritage, 23 Savile Row, London W1S 2ET
www.english-heritage.org.uk
English Heritage is the Government's statutory adviser on all aspects of the historic environment.

First published 2004

ISBN 1 873592 79 5
Product code 50921

*British Library Cataloguing in Publication Data*
A CIP catalogue record for this book is available from the British Library.

The National Monuments Record is the public archive of English Heritage. For more information contact NMR Enquiry and Research Services, National Monuments Record Centre, Kemble Drive, Swindon SN2 2GZ; telephone 01793 414600.

Brought to publication by René Rodgers and Andrew McLaren, Publishing, English Heritage, Kemble Drive, Swindon SN2 2GZ

Edited by Delia Gaze
Page layout by George Hammond
Printed in Northampton by Arkle Print

Northamptonshire County Council made a financial contribution towards the publication of this book.

# BUILT TO LAST?

The Buildings of the Northamptonshire Boot and Shoe Industry

Kathryn A Morrison with Ann Bond

Based on a survey directed by Adam Menuge

ENGLISH HERITAGE

Northamptonshire
County Council

# Contents

Frontispiece *Church's former factory, Duke Street, Northampton. The oldest block, built in 1877, is situated in the middle. The building to the right was acquired by Church's in the 1880s, and the unusually tall block on the left was erected in 1893. [BB99/05254]*

# Foreword

Northamptonshire has a world-wide reputation for high-quality boots and shoes founded in techniques and skills handed down from the middle of the 19th century. Then the county virtually shod the nation. If you were a soldier in the Great War you would most likely be wearing Northamptonshire boots, and at its peak the county produced as many shoes as did the rest of Great Britain put together. While maintaining its position at the top of the market, the pressures of the modern global economy since the 1950s have had a devastating impact on factories producing footwear for the wider public. This has led in recent years to a reduction in the scale of the industry and the loss of many of its distinctive buildings.

But not all is lost and this book documents and celebrates the extraordinary character of what survives. Because of the scale and particular history of the industry, shoemaking has created townscapes that are unique in England. And, because many of the historic buildings relating to the industry are robust and versatile, they can be put to new uses and given a fresh lease of life. Recent additions of boot and shoe buildings to the statutory lists indicate one way forward for the most important individual structures, but much of the character of these towns derives from a complex mix of factories, houses and workshops and the spaces between them. This calls for an imaginative strategic approach to whole areas if their distinctiveness is to be understood and sensitively managed. This book sets the scene and, we hope, by highlighting this rich Northamptonshire legacy, will help to ensure that as much of it as possible can be understood and enjoyed by generations to come.

Sir Neil Cossons
Chairman, English Heritage

Councillor Mick Young
Leader, Northamptonshire County Council

*The elaborate main entrance of William Barratt & Co's Footshape Boot Works on Kingsthorpe Road, Northampton. This eye-catching factory was built in 1913. [BB001833]*

Fig 1 *'The World Seeks our Products': these stained-glass doors in Fred Hawkes's shoe machinery factory on Portland Road, Rushden, built in the 1920s, illustrate the international importance of Northamptonshire's boot and shoe industry. [AA044187]*

# Introduction

Northamptonshire is renowned for the production of high-quality boots and shoes, particularly for men. Long-established manufacturers such as Church's, Crockett & Jones and Barker's are household names, not just in the United Kingdom, but also around the globe.

This international reputation is of long standing (Fig 1). Northampton was exporting boots and shoes as early as the 17th century, and the industry had spread to other parts of the county by 1850. At the zenith of the British Empire, Northamptonshire manufacturers despatched huge cargoes of boots and shoes – footwear for all climates and terrains – to the colonies. Periodically, the demands of war, from the Civil War (1642–8) to the Second World War (1939–45), spurred production to new heights and created new markets. In the First World War (1914–18) alone, Northampton manufacturers supplied the staggering number of 23 million pairs of boots and shoes to the Allied forces, while the rest of the county provided another 24 million pairs. To put this in context, other footwear-manufacturing areas of Great Britain produced only 23 million in total.

This thriving industry provided skilled employment for hundreds of thousands of people in Northamptonshire, generation after generation (Fig 2). It created wealth that enabled towns such as Kettering, Wellingborough and Rushden to expand at an unprecedented rate. New streets lined with factories and houses took the place of green fields, and it was impossible to escape the sights, sounds and smells of footwear manufacture.

The architectural inheritance of the boot and shoe industry (Fig 3), which defines the character of so many Northamptonshire towns, has been threatened for some time by the decline of the manufacture of mass-produced footwear in this country. Competition from the Continent and the Far East has accelerated since the end of the Second World War. This has affected not just Northamptonshire, but also other shoe-manufacturing centres, such as Leicester and Norwich. Although many well-known firms still produce high-quality footwear in

Fig 2 *Boot and shoe workers pose with a dog for the photographer in the factory yard at Parker & Howe's, 33 High Street, Long Buckby, about 1913. The village of Long Buckby specialised in the manufacture of long boots. [Northampton Museums and Art Gallery]*

Northamptonshire, sustaining its worldwide reputation, numerous businesses have folded, jobs have been lost and factories have closed. Regrettably, many significant buildings connected with the boot and shoe industry have been demolished; others lie empty and are vulnerable either to demolition or to damaging conversion. The importance of these buildings – in both national and local terms – has become more apparent as a result of a recent survey by English Heritage.

This book outlines the evolution of boot and shoe making in Northamptonshire. It describes the landscapes and buildings created in the service of the industry, highlights their special qualities, and emphasises the importance of conservation and regeneration in preserving what is best of the boot and shoe heritage for the future. Despite an increasing awareness that buildings connected with the industry constitute an irreplaceable resource, many of them are

Fig 3 *Although no longer used for its original purpose, this factory on Crabb Street in Rushden is well cared for and retains most of its original features, including its crane, loading doors and windows. It was built about 1887. [BB013242]*

insufficiently protected. The flexible spaces they contain offer great potential for sympathetic adaptation to new uses that can ensure the continuing vitality and quality of an area. Many of these buildings have enormous intrinsic value, and they all contribute to a highly distinctive urban environment of national importance. Furthermore, as experience in other historic industrial towns and cities demonstrates, buildings such as these have considerable commercial potential.

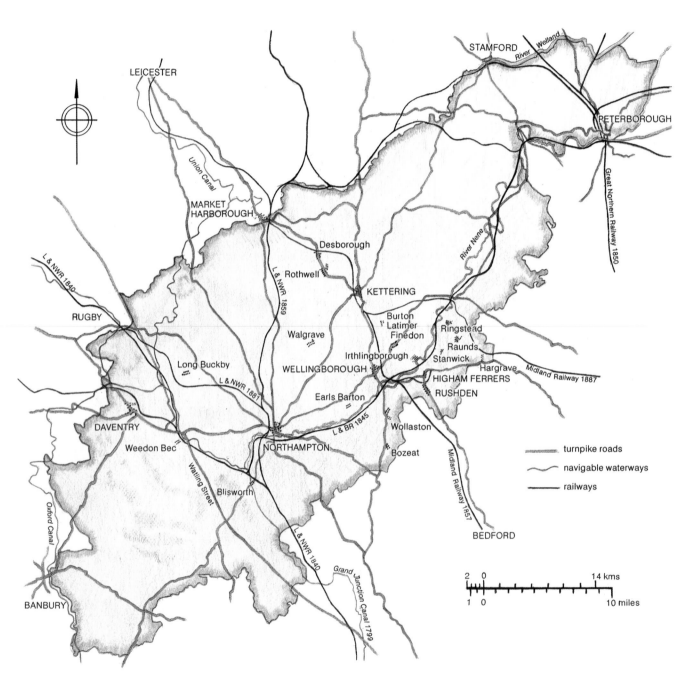

LEICESTER

STAMFORD

River Welland

PETERBOROUGH

Great Northern Railway 1850

Union Canal

MARKET
HARBOROUGH

Desborough

River Nene

L & NWR 1840

Rothwell

L & NWR 1859

KETTERING

Walgrave

Burton
Latimer
Finedon

Ringstead

RUGBY

Raunds

Irthlingborough

Stanwick

Hargrave

Midland Railway 1887

Long Buckby

L & NWR 1881

WELLINGBOROUGH

HIGHAM FERRERS

RUSHDEN

Earls Barton

DAVENTRY

L & BR 1845

Wollaston

Weedon Bec

NORTHAMPTON

Bozeat

Watling Street

Midland Railway 1857

Oxford Canal

Blisworth

BEDFORD

L & NWR 1840

Grand Junction Canal 1799

BANBURY

turnpike roads

navigable waterways

railways

2   0                    14 kms

1   0                    10 miles

# The landscape of the industry

Northamptonshire's boot and shoe towns (Figs 4 and 5) derive their distinctive character from the intimate relationship that existed between home-working (by 'outworkers') and factory production. This endured in shoemaking long after it had ceased to be of significance in other industries. Leather works and shoe factories were mixed with the workshops and terraced houses of workers, and often stood alongside the larger residences of managers and manufacturers. Despite the international reach of the industry, most of these buildings were designed by local architects and builders. They were modest in style, and rarely attempted to dominate their surroundings. As a result, they combine to create harmonious streetscapes, composed of well-proportioned, sturdy buildings, executed in local materials. Only the factories of the most ambitious manufacturers, and the commercial warehouses of the principal leather merchants, aspired to metropolitan grandeur.

The streetscapes of the boot and shoe industry did not develop their highly distinctive character until after 1850. Before then, warehouses and factories nestled discreetly behind manufacturers' houses, while most workers toiled in rooms in their houses rather than in purpose-built workshops.

As the industry expanded in the 1850s, 1860s and 1870s, new red-brick buildings were erected around the historic centre of Northampton, first to the north-west, then later to the north and north-east. While many streets to the north-west were cleared to make way for post-war redevelopment, those to the north and north-east remain largely intact (Fig 6). Similar developments were initiated after 1870 in towns such as Kettering, Rushden and Wellingborough. In Kettering they can be seen largely to the north-east of the town centre (*see* Fig 15), while in both Rushden and Wellingborough they are more evenly distributed around the heart of the old town. In all of these places this expansion took the form of straight streets lined by factories and terraced houses, interspersed with corner shops, schools, churches, chapels and working men's clubs. In Northampton, factories sometimes developed in

*Fig 4 This map depicts Northamptonshire about 1900 and identifies the main centres of boot and shoe manufacture. The spread of the boot and shoe industry throughout the county can be attributed to good communication systems, especially canals, navigable rivers, turnpike roads and the railway. Northampton itself, however, has had to rely on branch railway lines.*

### Kettering

Several impressive Victorian factories can be seen in the town. Factories still producing footwear include Ken Hall's and Loake's. Outworking was a particular feature of the local boot and shoe industry and single-storey garden workshops survive behind most of the terraced houses to the north and east of the town centre.

### Rushden

Rushden expanded hugely due to the growth of the boot and shoe industry in the late 19th century, and it has been compared to a 'goldrush' town. The historic core of the settlement is surrounded by late Victorian buildings, including many footwear factories. Working factories include Grenson's and Alfred Sargent's.

### Long Buckby

The village of Long Buckby specialised in the manufacture of long boots. Outworking – including a high proportion of hand sewing – continued into the 20th century, and many small workshops have survived.

### Northampton

Prestigious Northampton firms such as Church's, Tricker's and Crockett & Jones still manufacture footwear in premises of the late 19th and early 20th centuries. In some districts, the dense concentration of boot and shoe factories has created a predominantly industrial streetscape. Usually, however, factories are mixed with terraced housing and other buildings.

### Desborough

The co-operative movement influenced the development of the town and had a substantial interest in the boot and shoe industry. One former co-operative factory now manufactures leather handbags, and shoes are still made at Joseph Cheaney & Sons on Regent Street.

### Wellingborough

Shoemaking was of great importance in Wellingborough by the late 18th century. Ultimately, the town specialised in the production of uppers. Buildings relating to the industry – especially large workshops – survive throughout the town. Those still in production include J G Cox.

### Earls Barton

Boot and shoe factories are located at intervals throughout Earls Barton. A short distance from the historic settlement is the industrial suburb of New Barton. Laid out in the 1880s and 1890s, it is very different in character to the rest of Earls Barton and comprises a number of small boot and shoe factories and workers' housing.

### Raunds

Raunds is remembered for the Strike and March of 1905, when local boot and shoe makers marched to the War Office in London to present a petition demanding fair wages. Until 1939, 90 per cent of all boot and shoe work in the town was done under government contract, largely for the army and the navy. In recent years, many local factories have been demolished.

Fig 5 *This map shows the location of some of the most significant centres of boot and shoe manufacture in Northamptonshire.*

Fig 6 *The district shown in this aerial photograph, to the north-east of Northampton town centre, was built in the 1880s and 1890s. The large factory in the centre, belonging to Crockett & Jones, dominates the neighbourhood. Characteristically, the buildings were erected in regimented rows, and the predominant building material is red brick.*
*[NMR 23031/07 SP 7661/33]*

Fig 7 *This aerial view shows a dense cluster of factories at the junction of Overstone Road (left), Dunster Street (top) and St Michael's Road (bottom) in Northampton. Originally, these factories – built between the mid-1870s and late 1890s – belonged to Hornby & West, G T Hawkins and Collier's. A modern road, bottom left, runs through the site once occupied by Cove & West, whose factory was one of the most important in the town. [NMR 23032/08 SP 7560/58]*

clusters, or along one side of a street, creating industrial canyons: this can be observed most impressively on Henry Street, St Michael's Road (Fig 7) and Duke Street. At the end of the 19th century these red-brick streets must have presented a strong contrast to the historic core of the town, where most streets were lined with façades dating from the 18th and early 19th centuries, constructed in mellow local stone.

Greenery was scarce in boot and shoe districts, but in Kettering and many smaller towns, gardens and workshops could be glimpsed through narrow 'jitties' (the local term for alleys) and from corners, and were sometimes accessed by footpaths, or 'backways'. The workshops may have been largely hidden, but the occasional sounds of hammering or riveting would have contributed to the ambience of the streets. Another ingredient in the mix was the all-pervasive smell of leather.

In both towns and villages, the interdependence of factory work and outwork ensured that spaces for working existed close to spaces for living. Outworkers visited factories on a regular basis, to collect materials and to deliver finished products. Furthermore, factory workers lived as near as possible to their workplace, and liked to return home for dinner in the middle of each day. From the 1890s, when manufacturers began to erect single-storey factories on greenfield sites on the edges of towns, where land was plentiful and cheap, new housing quickly followed. Aside from the absence of garden workshops, the character of these footwear communities was not greatly different from those nearer town centres. The ideals of the garden suburb movement, however, can sometimes be detected in tree-lined streets and front gardens, and occasionally the factories themselves occupied a landscaped setting.

In many villages, boot and shoe communities were physically less close-knit than their urban counterparts, with workers coexisting with large (although decreasing) numbers of agricultural labourers. Their houses were less concentrated, and factories usually stood in splendid isolation. Nevertheless, urban-style developments were often planted somewhat incongruously in traditional village centres, or grafted on to their outskirts. This could take the form of red-brick terraces for factory hands or outworkers. In Long Buckby, Saunders Terrace (for factory hands) and Holyoake Terrace (for outworkers) both lie at right angles to

Fig 8 *A mixture of factories, houses and small workshops can be seen in this aerial view of Wollaston. The factories range in date from the Sheldon Factory of about 1900 (bottom right) to the Austin Factory of the 1920s (centre). To the north of the Austin Factory is Septimus Rivett's factory of 1915. [NMR 21992/07 SP 9162/8]*

the main street, and similar developments can be seen in Bozeat. Back lane factory development, running parallel to the main street, was erected in Irthlingborough (Victoria Street), Higham Ferrers (Midland Road) and Raunds (Park Road). More intricate boot and shoe suburbs, with a grid-plan of streets containing a mixture of factories and terraced houses, were built at New Barton (a suburb of Earls Barton), Wollaston (Fig 8) and Burton Latimer.

SHOEMAKING

# From craft to industry: history, processes and organisation

To understand the buildings and landscapes of the boot and shoe industry, it is necessary to know something about its history, and about the dramatic changes that occurred in the organisation of labour and in manufacturing processes over the centuries.

Before the 16th century Northamptonshire depended on wool for its wealth. Shoemaking (Figs 9 and 10), however, was already a significant trade. Master shoemakers worked with assistance from their families and two or three apprentices and journeymen (hired workmen). They produced bespoke boots and shoes, made to order for local customers, and ready-mades for a wider market. Before welted construction (*see* Fig 11) was introduced in the 16th century, most footwear was made by the turnshoe method, with uppers and soles sewn inside out, like pumps or garments. The shoemaker's main tools were knives, awls, hammers and lasts; his materials included thread, wax and, of course, leather.

The shoemaker procured his leather from the whitawer or currier. The currier treated tanned leather for its final use by softening it, shaving it and impregnating it with fats and oils. The currier, in turn, obtained his hides from the tanner, who prepared them by washing, dehairing, scraping, soaking, tanning in pits for a year or more, and then drying. As for the tanner, he generally bought hides from local butchers. Tanning was of considerable importance in medieval Northampton, because the town was surrounded by good grazing and had an ample supply of both water (for washing hides) and oak trees (for the bark used in the tanning process). Leather produced in the county was sold far afield, notably at Cambridge's famous Stourbridge Fair.

The boot and shoe industry (as opposed to the 'gentle craft' of traditional shoemaking) was well established by the time of the Civil War (1642–8), when a group of thirteen Northampton shoemakers, led by Thomas Pendleton, supplied the Parliamentarian Treasurers-at-War for Ireland with 4,000 pairs of shoes and 600 pairs of boots.

Fig 9 *(left) A Victorian image of 17th-century shoemaking in the Mayor's Balcony of Northampton Guildhall, built in 1864. This shoemaker is working near the window, sewing a sole. [AA044245]*

Fig 10 *This twin capital in the porch of Northampton Guildhall depicts a medieval shoe shop, as imagined by the Victorian sculptor. [AA044243]*

More orders followed, and Northampton continued to supply the army after the Restoration of the monarchy in 1660. By the early 18th century Northampton was known throughout England for its boots and shoes and was exporting footwear to the plantations of the West Indies.

Large orders could be met only by radically reorganising the industry. In this, the 'wholesale manufacturer' was pivotal. He employed shoemakers who continued to work in small groups, usually in their own homes. These shoemakers specialised in particular processes, such as closing (stitching together the components of uppers) or making (attaching uppers to soles). While the workshop of the medieval shoemaker had been located in the town centre, near the local market, shoemakers working on the wholesale system could live and work anywhere, so long as they were able to travel to and from the warehouse where the wholesale manufacturer stored his materials and finished products.

Northampton's success was possible because good communications linked it with London and major English ports. As well as being centres of distribution, by the mid-18th century ports had become focal points for the tanning industry. This happened as increasing quantities of hides had to be imported to meet demand. One significant side effect was the decline of the tanning industry in the Midlands, where numerous tanneries now closed down.

Despite their strategic advantages, Northampton shoemakers did not have a national monopoly. Most ready-made women's shoes were made in London garrets, and by the end of the 18th century a strong shoemaking industry had developed in Stafford, Norwich and Yorkshire (but not yet in Leicester). Northampton competed particularly well in the battle for the men's market because its shoemakers were prepared – or expected – to work for low wages. Indeed, business was driven out of London due to trade combinations demanding high wages, at precisely the time when turnpike roads and improved waterways were cutting the cost of transportation between London and provincial towns. The industry expanded to such an extent that wholesale manufacturers in Northampton sent large quantities of work ('basket work') to nearby villages. Demand for army boots was so great during the American War of Independence (1775–83) and the French Wars (1793–1815) that manufacturers now set up businesses in Kettering, Wellingborough and Daventry.

By the late 18th century some clickers and rough-stuff cutters, who cut out leather for uppers and soles respectively, were being employed in warehouses or manufactories rather than in their homes. This had great advantages. In particular, it enabled manufacturers to keep an eye on valuable raw materials, to discourage pilfering. Thus clickers and rough-stuff cutters became the first factory hands in the industry, and warehouses took their first step towards becoming factories. Unfortunately, we know so little as yet about specialist boot and shoe buildings from this period that we cannot say what they looked like, but they would certainly have been inconspicuous to passers-by.

Establishments described by contemporaries simply as 'factories' (as opposed to warehouses or manufactories) had come into being in Northampton by the 1830s. Most of these were run by 'small masters' – some of them women – who undertook certain processes, such as closing, on behalf of wholesale manufacturers. These factories were unmechanised and took advantage of cheap labour, employing children and journeymen. This provoked protests by shoemakers, who expressed their discontent by striking and picketing factories. This was as nothing, however, compared with the outrage caused by the introduction of closing machines – sewing machines adapted to stitch leather – in 1857. Although some machines had already been introduced to assist with particular shoemaking processes, such as presses for cutting leather, none had made a great impact. Closing machines, on the other hand, promised to revolutionise the industry and change the lives of shoemakers beyond all recognition. Closing had traditionally been women's work, and the operation of these machines was usually entrusted to female workers.

Initially, the mechanisation of the closing process in factories increased demand for outworkers who could carry out complementary (but slower) making processes, including hand sewing, riveting and pegging, at home. But from the 1860s the making processes, too, were overtaken by machinery (Fig 11) – notably by the Blake Sole Sewer, the Goodyear Welter and the Standard Screw Machine – and brought into the factory. By the end of the century lasting (pulling the closed upper over the last in preparation for sole attaching) and finishing (trimming, colouring, buffing and polishing the finished article) had also been mechanised and brought 'indoors' (into the factory). In this way, outworking declined as factories expanded. By the early 20th century outwork was largely restricted to the most skilled shoemakers, who continued to make considerable quantities of high-quality bespoke and orthopaedic footwear by hand. Ironically, many of those who abandoned their workshops for the factory floor were compelled to do so by the factory hands' union. In 1894 it brokered an agreement with manufacturers, stipulating that no processes were to be undertaken outside factories, except closing.

The industry grew in parallel with a mass market for ready-made footwear. Northamptonshire manufacturers relied on independent retailers to sell their goods until the 1880s, when, like Freeman, Hardy & Willis and Stead & Simpson in Leicester, they established their own chains of shops. Among the first in Northampton to pursue this route were Manfield (Fig 12) and J G Sears (True-Form). Occasionally this pattern of development was reversed by a footwear retailer expanding into manufacturing. William Timpson's chain of shoe shops, for example, was established a full decade before he opened his first workshop in Kettering in the 1880s. The Barratt family followed a different route. Beginning as retailers, in 1903 they established mail order as a novel means of marketing their goods. Customers unsure of their size appended a traced outline of their feet to their order, hence the name of the Footshape Boot Works (Fig 13; *see also* photo opposite Foreword), a landmark building on Kingsthorpe Road, Northampton.

In the late 19th and early 20th centuries, in the face of persistent competition from America, Northamptonshire continued to specialise in all qualities of men's footwear, while the production of children's and women's fashion footwear was concentrated in Leicester and Stafford, and high-quality women's shoes in Norwich. During the First World War, the range of footwear supplied by Northamptonshire to the Allied

Fig 11 *This diagram identifies the principal parts of a man's boot, made of welted construction. It is surrounded by illustrations of machines used in the boot and shoe industry:*
*a) a Blake Sole Sewer;*
*b) a Standard Screw Machine;*
*c) a Singer sewing machine, used to sew uppers; and*
*d) a Goodyear Welt Machine. [Based on archive photographs]*

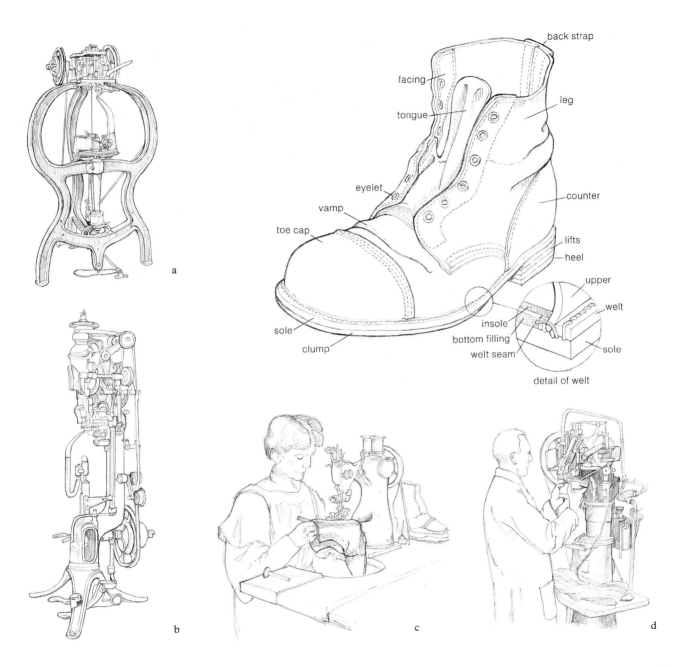

back strap

facing

tongue

leg

eyelet

vamp

counter

toe cap

lifts

heel

sole

upper

welt

clump

insole

bottom filling

welt seam

sole

detail of welt

a

b

c

d

SHOES OF BESPOKE CHARACTER

Fig 12 *A model window display created for Manfield's shops emphasises the 'bespoke character' of the shoes, which would have been manufactured in Manfield's Northampton factory. [Northampton Museums and Art Gallery]*

forces was enormous, including Russian Cossack boots, rope-soled boots for the tank corps, submarine deck boots and mosquito boots, as well as the standard B5 British infantry boot (similar to the boot depicted in Fig 11).

By the 1920s the industry was in decline. The domestic market was saturated, and important export markets were lost to foreign competition, especially from the Czechoslovakian firm Bata. Several businesses tried switching to the manufacture of women's fashion shoes during the Depression, but many went on short time or simply closed. The Second World War brought something of a reprieve, with most factories returning to the manufacture of army boots. After 1945 manufacturers invested heavily in new processes using adhesives and plastics. However, this happened just as competition was intensifying. Numerous factories and high-street retail chains, including Sears, were bought by Charles Clore, who formed the British Shoe Corporation. Clore, a property magnate, was more interested in retailing than

Fig 13 *Barratt's Footshape Boot Works in Northampton was designed by the specialist shoe-factory architect Alexander Ellis Anderson and opened in 1913. The lettering on the neo-baroque front range, which served as a conspicuous advertisement for the company, was inspired by Castle Ashby, a country house 17.5 kilometres from Northampton. Barratt's closed in 1997, and the single-storey factory, located behind the front range, was demolished following a serious fire. [BB001829]*

manufacture, and began to stock his shops with inexpensive shoes from developing countries. British shoe factories could not compete and, despite desperate attempts at rationalisation, many went out of business.

But all was not lost. Increased affluence in the 1980s and 1990s brought a revival in demand for high-quality men's shoes, and many of the county's most successful companies are those that have continuously pursued that specialist, high-value market. This emphasises the importance of traditional shoemaking in maintaining Northamptonshire's international status.

Boot and shoe manufacture has had a long and profitable history in Northamptonshire. As we will see, however, it was in the relatively short period between 1870 and 1920 that the industry made its biggest impression on the built environment of villages and towns throughout the county.

## Buildings of the boot and shoe industry

A wide range of different buildings has been erected to serve the Northamptonshire boot and shoe industry in the course of the last 150 years. These buildings include the small workshops of outworkers, larger workshops designed to accommodate teams of workers, boot and shoe factories, leather works, warehouses, machinery works and last works. It must be remembered that none of these different building types functioned independently, but that they relied on one another for their economic well-being.

### Outworkers' workshops

Every boot and shoe factory depended to some degree on outworkers before the 1890s, and it is important to realise that much of the work that contributed to Northamptonshire's international reputation was carried out in simple artisan dwellings. Before the 1860s, the workshop of a boot and shoe outworker would have occupied part of a room in his house, usually a corner of a living room or bedroom. All he required was sufficient light to work by, a source of heat (to warm wax and glue, as well as himself), and enough space for a chair or stool, hand tools and materials. A bench would have been necessary if the work entailed riveting. Within the domestic workplace, the outworker could vary his hours, discuss politics with friends and involve his wife and children in his work, while his employer had the advantage of being able to supply him with work according to demand. Both parties lost a high degree of flexibility once the factory system began to supersede outworking.

After 1860 new working-class houses often incorporated a workshop, especially in districts where boot and shoe outworking was common. This represented a distinct improvement in workers' conditions. Whether detached or not, a dedicated workshop distanced the smell and mess of the various processes from the domestic sphere. Outworkers' workshops were sometimes built for specific tenants, but were usually erected by manufacturers as an integral part of new residential schemes. Many of the houses and workshops built after 1890, especially in villages, were provided by manufacturing co-operative societies (Fig 14).

Fig 14 *A pair of workshops, showing a shoemaker at work. This drawing is based on a survey of the workshop behind 57 East Street, Long Buckby, which was built by a local co-operative society about 1890. As well as a workshop, each outbuilding accommodated a coal house and a privy.*

Fig 15 *An aerial photograph of Wood Street and Havelock Street in Kettering, showing late 19th-century factories interspersed with terraced housing. Outworkers' workshops can be seen in many of the narrow gardens. [NMR 23034/19 SP 8679/3]*

Strangely, outworking does not seem to have influenced the layout of new residential developments in Northampton, except for a few streets north of Billing Road, where much of the evidence has gone. Some detached single-person workshops were erected on an ad hoc basis behind terraced houses. This can be seen in the Phippsville area of the town – built in the late Victorian and Edwardian periods – where workshops could be accessed from long alleys. Most Northampton workshops, however, remained invisible and inaccessible from the streets.

In contrast to Northampton, individual outworking was common in Kettering, which specialised in cheap riveted boots for labourers. As many as 2,000 small, detached workshops survive in the town, with a particular concentration in the Havelock Street and Wood Street district (Fig 15), which was largely developed by the local manufacturers William Meadows and John Bryan between 1876 and 1883. There, back

Fig 16 (above, left) Kettering workshops viewed through a 'jitty', or 'tunnel', running through a row of terraced houses. [AA044198]

Fig 17 (above, right) This row of workshops lies behind a terrace which sits at right angles to New Street in Rothwell. The houses and workshops are served by separate footpaths. Most of these workshops are now used simply as garden sheds, but notice the remains of the brick chimney stacks. [AA044165]

alleys and 'tunnel-back' terraces (Fig 16) enhanced communications between garden workshops and factories. The single-storey brick workshops abut the rear walls of gardens behind the terraced houses. They usually have a monopitch roof, a corner or rear-wall fireplace or stove, and a large timber-framed window overlooking the garden. Most of the Kettering workshops date from the 1880s, although some are clearly older. The outworking system entered a decline in the 1890s, but garden workshops continued to be built in Kettering until at least 1913 – much later than in comparable industries such as wool and cotton – and many were still being used for their original purpose in the 1960s.

Single-storey, detached workshops like those in Kettering can be found throughout the county (Fig 17), although not in such a dense concentration. Another distinct type of workshop was built over a store and/or privy. The main benefit of this arrangement was that the first-floor workshop admitted more light than a ground-level one.

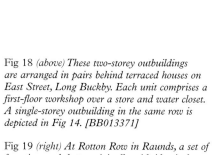

Fig 18 *(above) These two-storey outbuildings are arranged in pairs behind terraced houses on East Street, Long Buckby. Each unit comprises a first-floor workshop over a store and water closet. A single-storey outbuilding in the same row is depicted in Fig 14. [BB013371]*

Fig 19 *(right) At Rotton Row in Raunds, a set of four tiny workshops, originally with identical windows, occupies the first floor of a lean-to, built against the gable end of a short terrace. Each workshop had its own entrance and ladder stair. [AA026814]*

Fig 20 *Crispin Cottages in Walgrave were named after St Crispin, the patron saint of shoemakers. The terrace bears a datestone reading 'SW 1895'. The initials belonged to Stephen Norton Walker, whose shoe factory on Walker's Acre – recently converted into flats – was the only one in the village. Undoubtedly, Walker employed outworkers who worked in the 'cottage shoe shops' attached to the rear of the houses. [AA044182]*

Fig 21 *A rear-range workshop at 20 Bailiff Street and Robert Street, Northampton, probably built for a machine closer about 1870. The house lies to the left. The three-storey building to the right was erected as a factory in 1869, but has been converted to residential use. [AA026830]*

Particularly well-preserved examples behind East Street in Long Buckby (Fig 18) were built by a local co-operative society about 1890, and extended in 1898. While most workshops of this type were detached, a row of four first-floor workshops in Raunds (Fig 19) was built against the end of a terrace. Single-storey workshops attached to individual houses, yet another variation on this adaptable building type, were more common. In the village of Walgrave, for example, workshops usually abutted the sides or backs of houses. Those behind Crispin Cottages (Fig 20), a four-house terrace on Baker's Lane, were built in 1895, but after 1900 it became increasingly rare for new houses to incorporate working space in this manner.

## Large workshops

Another distinct building type associated with the boot and shoe industry is the large workshop, designed to accommodate a team rather than a solitary worker. These were usually attached to or integrated within ordinary houses and were considerably smaller than most boot and shoe factories. They were usually managed by the owner or occupier of the adjoining house. This arrangement may have originated in the first half of the 19th century. Early examples might have been created by adding rear extensions to houses, but by the 1860s designs for new houses were being modified to incorporate large workshops from the outset (Fig 21).

Most large workshops were occupied by 'small masters', also known as 'manufacturers to the trade', essentially sub-contractors who employed people to carry out particular processes for wholesale manufacturers. Some ran machine-closing concerns. The master would have rented sewing machines and employed teenage girls and women to operate them. There was no need for power, and investment was minimal. Some workshops, however, were occupied by manufacturers who either operated on a very small scale or were just starting up in business. While those who were successful soon moved to a larger site, and usually to a purpose-built factory, others were able to expand from their original premises. One such firm was Tebbutt & Hall Bros, whose workshop on Coleman Street in Raunds was extended in piecemeal fashion over sixty years, and eventually became a large factory. It was demolished in 2001.

Large workshops were particularly common in Northampton, where material evidence for individual outworking after 1870 is slight. Workshops (Fig 22) were usually located in a first-floor room, over the (larger than normal) rear range of a terraced house, and they had their own separate entrance and staircase. Access was determined by position: most were located on corner sites, and had a domestic entrance on the front elevation and a workers' entrance on the side. Those located in the middle of terraces had two front doors, one giving directly into the house, the other to the workshop at the rear. Both types are easily recognisable, and many examples can be seen on Northampton streets developed in the 1860s, 1870s and 1880s. Comparable workshops can be found in other towns in the county, such as Wellingborough.

A number of large workshops and small factories took the form of detached buildings (Fig 23), erected on gardens behind houses rather than being incorporated within their footprint. These were usually, but not inevitably, in the same ownership or occupation as the house. Some achieved a considerable size, but, as part of the local streetscape, they remained less visible than the stand-alone factories of the wholesale boot and shoe manufacturers.

## Boot and shoe factories

The roots of the Northamptonshire boot and shoe industry can be traced to the 16th century, yet factories erected before 1870 do not survive in significant numbers. The first manufactories (buildings where work was carried out) evolved from earlier warehouses (buildings where materials were stored), and for a period in the middle of the 19th century the two terms, 'factory' and 'warehouse', were used interchangeably. The little information we possess about early factories comes from documents. Deeds and advertisements reveal that the standard arrangement, involving rough-stuff cutting on the ground floor or basement, and clicking on upper floors, was well established by 1850. This endured in multi-storey factories until the 1890s and was modified only as new processes, such as closing and making, were brought indoors.

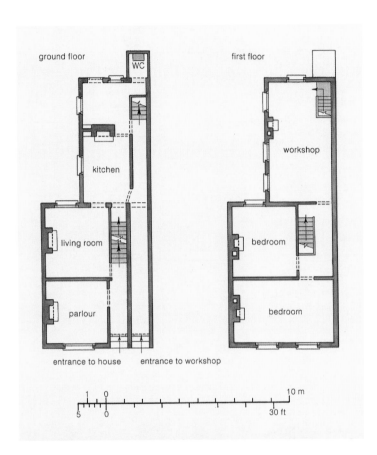

ground floor              first floor

WC

kitchen

workshop

living room              bedroom

parlour               bedroom

entrance to house   entrance to workshop

1   0                10 m

5   0                30 ft

Fig 22 (above) A small first-floor workshop formed part of 53 Alcombe Road, Northampton, which is a mid-terrace house. The workshop had its own staircase, approached through a separate entrance and a passage that ran along the side of the property. This has now been incorporated within the house. [Redrawn from a survey by Brian Giggins]

Fig 23 (right) A small, detached factory of the 1860s or 1870s hides behind an end-of-terrace house at the west end of Havelock Street, Kettering. [AA044173]

Factories dating from the 1850s and 1860s are rare and of considerable interest. They include the former Trafalgar Works (Fig 24) on Sheep Street, Wellingborough, which shares the street frontage with the house of the owner, Nathaniel Pearce Sharman. A similar arrangement can be seen at 3 New Street, Daventry, premises belonging to John Line (later Line & Cattell), where a double-pile warehouse or factory was built alongside an earlier house. These two sites represent a new departure, since maps of the period suggest that most factories were situated behind houses, lying at right angles – rather than parallel – to the street. This latter pattern of development can still be seen in other industrial towns, such as the Jewellery Quarter of Birmingham.

From the 1850s it became usual for the factories of wholesale boot and shoe manufacturers to occupy the street frontages of sites, rather than hiding behind houses. Most conspicuous of all were the two 'monster' factories built in Northampton for Moses Philip Manfield and Isaac, Campbell & Co. In each case work began in 1857, coinciding with the introduction of the town's first closing machines and causing considerable alarm. While Manfield – a decent and trusted employer – assured local shoemakers that he was building a warehouse rather than a factory, Isaac, Campbell & Co made no secret of its plan to install closing machines. Before either factory opened, however, closing machines had been adopted in other shoe towns, persuading Manfield to change his mind. He became one of twenty local manufacturers who published their resolve to install the machines without delay. Industrial action followed, but had no effect. Workers held out for a couple of months, then bowed to the inevitable.

Isaac, Campbell's and Manfield's factories (Fig 25) both opened in 1859. They were located side-by-side on Campbell Square and were demolished in 1982. The huge factory belonging to Isaac, Campbell & Co was designed by William Hull. It had an ornate office block on the corner of Campbell Square and Victoria Street, and much plainer rear ranges. In this factory, both closing and (more unusually) making were brought indoors. The women employed to operate closing machines had their own separate workrooms, entrances, staircases and water closets. Initially, much of the men's work was unmechanised. In what appears to

Fig 24 *Sharman's shoe factory (left) and house (right) of about 1850, on Sheep Street, Wellingborough. Unlike most later factories, this building is of stone, and originally had sash glazing. [AA044212]*

Fig 25 *The demolition of the Northampton factories of Isaac, Campbell's (left, on corner) and Manfield's (right, with 'campanile') in 1982 is a matter of regret. Our understanding of the boot and shoe industry has improved immeasurably in the last twenty years, and we have learnt to appreciate this kind of industrial landmark. [BB82/7720]*

Fig 26 *Hornby & West's factory was built on the corner of Overstone Road and St Michael's Road, Northampton, in 1876, and extended in 1883 and 1893; it was taken over by its neighbour, G T Hawkins Ltd, about 1912. The building was used for shoemaking into the 1990s. (See also* Fig 7.*)* [BB001586]

Fig 27 (top) In Kettering, several purpose-built footwear factories of the 1870s adopted a distinctive Italianate style. These included Spence & Page's Compton Works, erected on Field Street in 1878 and later extended to the left. The building has been converted into housing. [BB018467]

Fig 28 (bottom) This mid-Victorian factory on Palmerston Road, Northampton, has an unusual elevation in a reduced version of Venetian Gothic, with a giant order carrying pointed arches. The particularly large windows were retained when the building – now Palmerston House – was converted into flats. [BB018419]

have been a new system, perhaps of American origin, shoemakers were arranged in teams of twelve, with four seated around each table.

Manfield's building made a much more powerful architectural statement. The unknown architect adopted an Italianate *palazzo* style, imitating the great commercial warehouses of London and industrial cities. Since Manfield's and Isaac, Campbell's – like so many other early shoe warehouses and factories – have gone, the earliest surviving shoe factory in Northampton may be the very simple building at 3–5 Robert Street, which was built in 1869 for a short-lived shoemaking co-operative.

Few of the boot and shoe factories built after 1870 were as decorative or as large as the 'monster' factories. Most were of local red or orange brick, with Welsh slate roofs (Fig 26). Decoration was restricted to doorways, window heads and cornices, although small stone reliefs and inscriptions were occasionally set into façades. In the 1870s the Italianate style was particularly popular in Kettering (Fig 27). It was usually enlivened by polychromy, which was favoured well into the 1890s. On the whole, footwear manufacturers did not opt for the Gothic style, but at least one factory in Northampton combined pier-and-panel construction with pointed arches to striking effect (Fig 28). A handful of buildings were influenced by the Arts and Crafts aesthetics of the late 1880s and 1890s, while a larger number had neo-Jacobean features, such as shaped gables and stone bands. As for size, factories were typically two or, more usually, three storeys high, anything from three to eighteen bays long, and had rectangular, T-shaped or L-shaped plans. Most were built at the instigation of manufacturers, but a few were clearly built speculatively. The Northampton builder Henry Martin, for example, was responsible for erecting several attached pairs of factories in the town.

Structurally, footwear factories were uncomplicated. In the early 1870s they were often so narrow, and housed so little weighty machinery above ground level, that there was no need to support the floors with an internal row of columns. Floor beams and roof trusses were of timber, with simple chamfers on their undersides. These buildings had flat- or segmental-headed windows, fitted with wooden

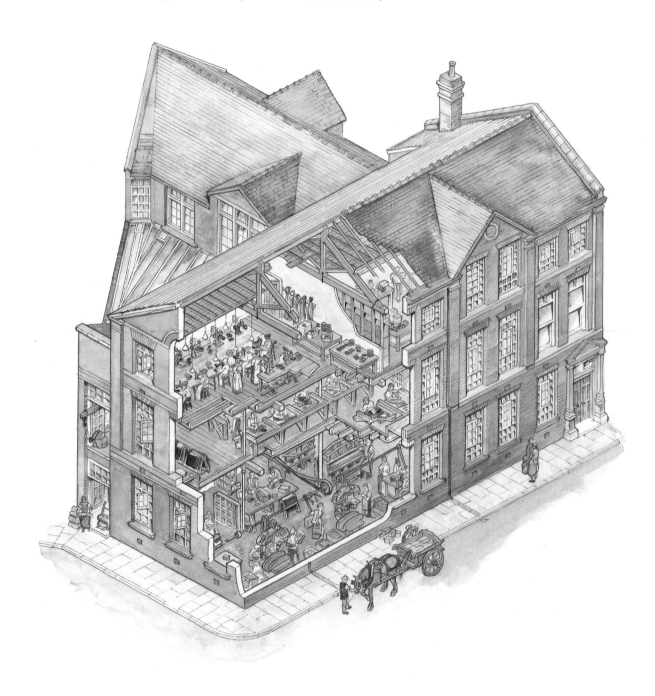

Fig 29 *(left) G T Hawkins's Northampton factory was designed by Charles Dorman and erected in 1886 on the corner of Overstone Road and Dunster Street (see Fig 7). It had a rough-stuff shop and riveters' shop on the ground floor, with clickers' rooms and a small closing room on the upper floors. The name of the factory's most famous product, 'Waukerz' footwear, is displayed over the office doorway.*

Fig 30 *The Havelock Works of Kettering Co-operative Boot and Shoe Manufacturing Society was built in 1890: note the relief and motto on the oriel window. Factories often occupied corner sites to obtain maximum lighting. In such cases it was common for the corner bay to contain a prestigious entrance leading to offices, which is the arrangement here. [BB001992]*

sash or cast-iron glazing. Most had loading (or 'taking-in') doors, served by iron cranes or winches, known as 'lifts'. Cranes were used principally to raise leather from horse-drawn drays to upper-floor clicking rooms and materials stores.

By the mid-1870s the typical factory was of pier-and-panel construction, with separate entrances for offices and workers, at least one loading door and vehicular access to a small, rear yard, which sometimes contained a stable. The tall windows that lit the factory floors were usually fitted with cast-iron glazing, incorporating hopper openings for ventilation (*see* Fig 55), while roofs carried skylights or ridge lanterns with louvred sides. The glass in the windows was reeded (or frosted), preventing workers from looking out and providing an evenly diffused light for them to work by. Improved natural and artificial lighting enabled interiors gradually to become deeper, at first being divided by a single row of cast-iron columns, but by the late 1880s comprising three or more aisles. From that time, perhaps as machinery was installed on upper storeys, but more likely as a simple response to structural advances, iron or steel I-section beams were used increasingly for floor construction. From the 1890s stone or concrete stairs were enclosed within fireproof compartments: a great advance on the open-sided wooden 'ladder stairs' of earlier years. Full steel framing was not used for footwear factory construction until the years immediately preceding the First World War.

In terms of function, factories were very simple (Fig 29). A small office suite existed, with facilities for the reception of outworkers and for the travellers who came to Northamptonshire to examine samples and order products from the factories. Offices were usually located on the first floor, towards the front of the building. From the outside, they can be recognised by their wooden-framed sash windows (Fig 30), which often contrast with the cast-iron-framed windows of the factory floors. They were served by a separate entrance and an enclosed staircase. Most offices had a waiting area, a small clerk's office with a glazed front and a private office with a fireplace. The principal office sometimes had a bay window, which enhanced the view of the delivery and despatch area. Offices were served by their own water closet, quite separate from that used by the factory hands.

The main processes carried out on factory floors were rough-stuff cutting and clicking. Rough-stuff cutters (Fig 31) were positioned in the basement or on the ground floor because they used heavy presses. Clickers (Fig 32), who cut leather by hand, were generally accommodated on upper floors, since their main requirement was copious light. Some buildings were laid out with small open areas or yards on all sides, just so that clickers could benefit from as many windows as possible. The clickers stood at benches facing the windows, with storage racks or tables arranged behind them.

When processes other than rough-stuff cutting and clicking were brought indoors, such as closing (Fig 33), there was no universal system to govern their positions. Rooms for sole sewers were generally located close to the rough-stuff department. Riveters and lasters were often placed in single-storey rooms with top-lighting. Finishing rooms (Fig 34) were usually located either on the ground floor or, less often, on the upper floor. Processes seldom flowed through a building in a straightforward manner, either downwards or upwards. The location of different departments depended on the weight of the machinery involved and the strength of the floors. As a result of these practical

*Fig 31 (above, left) Manfield's rough-stuff department, with revolution presses for bottom-stock cutting, in the 1920s. At this stage, the different components of boots and shoes were carried around the factory in wicker baskets, which can be seen in the foreground. Pattern racks can be seen against the far wall. [Northampton Museums and Art Gallery]*

*Fig 32 (above, right) The clicking room in Sears' True-Form factory in Northampton in the early 1900s. Clickers had a higher social status than other boot and shoe workers, because their work was so skilled. Note the open space of the factory floor. [Northampton Museums and Art Gallery]*

Fig 33 *(above, left) Most of the women who worked in boot and shoe factories were employed in closing rooms, sewing uppers with machines. They were kept quite separate from male workers, but were often supervised by a male foreman. This closing room formed part of G M Tebbutt's Grove Works on Grove Road, Northampton, and was photographed in 1924. The women in the centre of the room appear to be lasting. [Courtesy of Colin Clayson; BB029607]*

Fig 34 *(above, right) The finishing room of Manfield's Northampton factory in the 1920s, with men buffing shoes in the foreground. Note the large dust extractor in the background. Once shoes were fully assembled they were transported around the factory in wheeled racks rather than baskets. [Northampton Museums and Art Gallery]*

considerations, materials and footwear travelled up and down the building, in baskets or on trolleys, as they moved from one production stage to the next. Factories installed hoists and chutes to facilitate the flow between departments, and by 1914 some manufacturers had installed electric lifts.

On each floor of the factory, since the principal requirement was unobstructed working space, internal partitions and light wells were kept to a minimum. The foreman, or supervisor, had an unimpeded view from his workplace at one end of the room, but by the end of the century he was usually allocated a private office, constructed of lightweight partitions fitted with large windows. Each floor was served by one or two water closets and a 'lavatory' (washroom), projecting into the yard in the form of a sanitary annex. Some factories provided a cloakroom on each floor, where workers could hang their hats and coats; otherwise coat pegs were provided within the workspace (*see* Fig 32). Such details are very evocative, reminding us of the daily habits of the men and women whose working lives were passed in these buildings.

Factories were heated by hot-water pipes, which were either suspended from beams or ran around the edges of rooms (*see* Fig 55).

Businesses with a strong export trade often required a drying room with hot-water pipes capable of being heated to 150 degrees Fahrenheit (65.5 degrees Celsius); this prevented mildew developing when the product was in transit. Daylight was augmented by gas lighting, which was in general use before 1858, when particular mention was made of the fact that Gotch's factory in Kettering was fitted with gas throughout. Although gas was superseded by electricity in some factories by 1890, gas lights can still be seen in photographs taken after the First World War (see Fig 33), and some gas pipes and jets remain in situ today. The drive shafts, wheels and belts that ran the machinery were either suspended from mountings attached to beams or fixed to the walls. Motive power was produced by steam or gas engines; generally, these were located in the basement or on the ground floor. Steam and gas engines continued to be used for some time after electric motors became viable at the beginning of the 20th century.

Although multi-storey factories were built into the 20th century, a more practical factory model – laid out on one storey – presented itself to Northamptonshire footwear manufacturers in the early 1880s. The single-storey factory had been adopted in other industries and was already favoured by United States competitors in the shoe trade. Closer to home, a factory of this type was built for Birdsall's, a Northampton bookbinder, in 1882: it featured in *The Builder* of January 1883, and shortly afterwards a number of similar structures were erected as additions to existing boot and shoe factories. Hornby & West in Northampton, for example, built a single-storey riveting room with five parallel aisles in 1883. But it was some time before a new footwear factory was built entirely on this principle. The first is generally thought to have been Manfield's gigantic new factory, which opened on Wellingborough Road, Northampton, in 1892 (see Figs 31, 34 and 40). Manfield's, however, was preceded by the more modest Albion Works in Stamford Road, Kettering, which opened before 1891. The single-storey factory is an extremely vulnerable building type: the Albion Works has been demolished, and all that remains of Manfield's is the street range, making surviving Victorian and Edwardian footwear factories of this type all the more rare (Fig 35).

Fig 35 *A Lee's Enterprise Factory was built on Bective Road, Northampton, in 1902. The north-facing slopes of the sawtooth roofs contain skylights.* [BB013273]

The only elements of this new type of factory that could rise to two or more storeys or receive architectural elaboration were the entrance block and the manager's house. The style of façades varied enormously, some being severely simple, others fairly ornate. As in earlier factories, offices occasionally incorporated a bay or oriel window that overlooked the main entrance. Inside, they were separated from the factory floor by glazed partitions, which facilitated supervision of the workforce. Upper-floor rooms in entrance blocks were sometimes used for the storage of leather or finished shoes. Other rooms could include a dining room, but rarely a kitchen, demonstrating that workers were expected to bring their own midday meal. This, together with the provision of bicycle sheds, was perhaps an indication of the distance some workers now travelled to work.

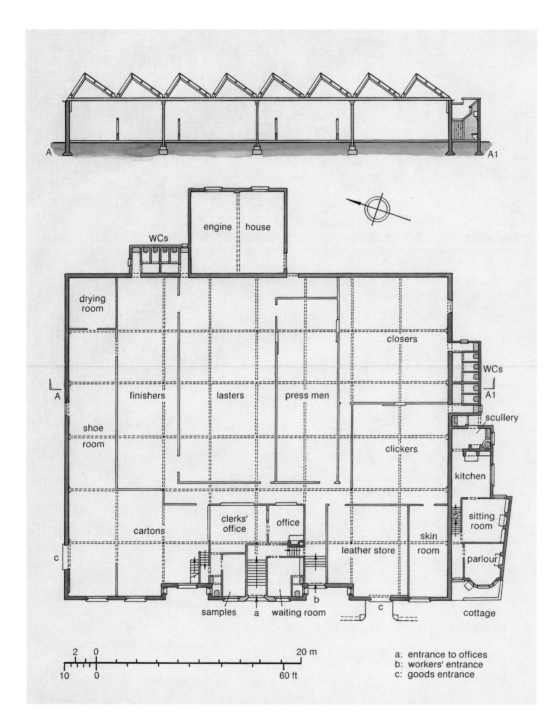

A

A1

WCs

engine house

drying room

closers

WCs

A

finishers

lasters

press men

A1

shoe room

scullery

clickers

kitchen

cartons

clerks' office

office

sitting room

skin room

leather store

parlour

c

samples

a

waiting room

b

c

cottage

2  0

20 m

10  0

60 ft

a: entrance to offices
b: workers' entrance
c: goods entrance

Fig 36 *The factory of F T Tebbutt & Co, Countess Road, Northampton, was designed by Walter Shaw in 1902. The building has been demolished, but this very clear plan helps us to understand how single-storey footwear factories functioned. The manager's house stood to one side. [Redrawn from Northampton Building Plan G148, Northamptonshire Record Office]*

Behind the entrance block, the single-storey factory floor was generally built with a combination of iron and steel until the years immediately preceding the First World War, when full steel frames became increasingly common. There was little to distinguish these structures from factories built to serve other industries. Their chief benefit was that heavy machinery could be concentrated at ground level. In addition, spacious departments could be covered with minimal obstruction and received copious light from above. While some factories had asymmetrical roofs fitted with north-facing skylights, others had symmetrical roofs with ridge lanterns or skylights.

Departments were arranged so that processes followed one another in a rational order around the building (Fig 36), with raw materials coming in at one end and the final product being despatched at the other. This was already evident at the Albion Works, which had two gateways in the front elevation, one for inward goods, the other for outward goods. As in most footwear factories, there were two entrances for the workpeople: one for the women who worked in the closing and finishing rooms, and another for the men. Workrooms were divided from one another by light, glazed partitions (at least 2.5 metres high), which could easily be moved if departments expanded or contracted. Electric lighting and gas or electric power, rather than steam, were now common. The shoe machinery was leased from a number of different suppliers, many of whom were based in the county.

Fires were a regular occurrence in the boot and shoe industry, and awareness of fire safety was heightened by a series of disastrous conflagrations in the late 19th and early 20th centuries, for example at John Cave's Rushden factory in 1877 and 1901. By the early 20th century standard fire equipment included sprinkler systems and iron-plated fire doors (Fig 37). Some large factories, including Hawkins' and Sears', had water towers (erected in 1908 and 1909 respectively), which housed the header tank for the sprinkler system. Fire escape stairs were another common addition in the years leading up to the First World War.

Despite the convenience of the single-storey factory, the multi-storey factory was never completely abandoned. In fact, the advent of

Fig 37 *A Mather & Platt fire door in G T Hawkins's Northampton factory, separating the office suite from the production floor. It was installed in 1915.* [AA044154]

Fig 38 *The premises of Crockett & Jones were built in a number of phases between 1889 and 1935. This four-storey block with basement, which dominates adjoining terraced housing on Turner Street, Northampton, was designed by Brown & Mayor and built in 1910. It was probably the first steel-framed building in the town. [AA044180]*

Fig 39 *(right, top) Tricker's originated in London, but moved to Northampton in 1903. The factory at 54–60 St Michael's Road has an unusual glazed brick façade, erected in 1924. The firm still employs about 70 people who make 700 pairs of shoes a week. It supplies the Royal Household and is entitled to use the coat of arms of the Prince of Wales. [AA044206]*

Fig 40 *(right, bottom) This aerial photograph shows (to bottom left) the CWS factory on Christchurch Road, Northampton, built in 1923–4 and now successfully reused for a range of light industrial businesses. All three CWS shoe factories in Northamptonshire were designed by the CWS architect, L G Ekins. Top right, the surviving front range of Manfield's Wellingborough Road factory of 1892, one of the first factories in the town to be listed, can be glimpsed. [NMR 23033/01 SP 7761/26]*

steel framing, reinforced concrete and efficient lifts encouraged something of a revival, and between 1910 and 1939 several highly modern, flat-roofed factories and factory extensions were built with three or four floors. These were constructed on the so-called daylight principle, with windows that filled the entire space between structural piers. The earliest factory of this type, and the best survival, is Crockett & Jones's extension of 1910 (Fig 38), designed by Brown & Mayor. This was probably the first steel-frame building in Northampton. The consummate example, however, was William Timpson's factory, erected on Bath Road, Kettering, in 1922, but demolished in 1972. The building had such large windows that it acquired the nickname 'Crystal Palace'. Employees had use of a canteen and sports fields, facilities that were offered only by a handful of enlightened boot and shoe manufacturers. Another innovative building of the 1920s was Sears' factory extension of 1925 on Stimpson Avenue, Northampton, designed by F H Allen. The novelty of this building – recently converted to residential use – concerned the use of drawn steel wire rather than rolled steel rods in the reinforced concrete floors and roofs. The inner walls of such factories, being little more than piers between windows, were clad in glazed white tiles, which enhanced the brightness of the interiors.

In comparison with previous decades, very few new factories were erected in the 1920s (Figs 39 and 40). The most notable single-storey factories of the decade were built in Northampton and Wellingborough by the Co-operative Wholesale Society (CWS), which had already erected a large factory in Rushden before the First World War. The CWS produced good footwear at reasonable prices, and had a dependable market in the shops of co-operative retail societies, while other manufacturers struggled to find an outlet for their goods. After the Depression, some factories were built in an impressive Modern style. The most outstanding of these was erected in 1938 for John White (Impregnable Boots) Ltd on Higham Road, Rushden (Fig 41). It was designed by Sir Albert Richardson, and may have been the first and only footwear factory in the county to be floodlit at night. Factories built since 1945 – ranging from Barker's hutted extension of 1950 to

R Griggs & Co's hi-tech building of 2000 (Fig 42) – are essentially utilitarian and seldom exhibit the panache of their predecessors.

It is clear that Northamptonshire manufacturers made their biggest capital investment in buildings between the years 1870 and 1920. They entrusted this work to locally based architects with a specialist knowledge of the industry and its requirements. Prominent among these men were Charles Dorman in the late 19th century, Alexander Ellis Anderson in the early 20th and, to a lesser extent, F H Allen between the wars. Stylistically, the taste of Northamptonshire manufacturers was conventional, but they were always willing to embrace new approaches when it came to the construction and arrangement of their factory buildings. Large numbers of these buildings still stand as a testimony to their entrepreneurial flair and as an integral part of the built landscape of Northamptonshire.

## Buildings for the leather trade

Northamptonshire had numerous leather-dressing factories and wholesale leather warehouses, but surprisingly few tanneries. Although tanning had been of relatively little importance in the county since the mid-18th century, a large new tannery (Figs 43 and 44) was built for W Pearce at Billing Park, outside Northampton, in the years 1937–9. Designed by Wilfrid Lawson Carter, it occupied spacious landscaped grounds and is among the most attractive 20th-century industrial buildings in the county. A relatively small percentage of its output, however, was destined for the local boot and shoe industry.

Leather dressing, traditionally known as currying, became a significant trade in Northamptonshire in the middle of the 19th century. After 1850 curriers deployed a growing range of presses and other machines to produce a wide variety of finishes, including calf kid, coloured 'Russian' leather and patent leather. Most – but not all – of this leather was sold to boot and shoe manufacturers.

Curriers bought ready-tanned leather from suppliers in London and other ports, but often had pits for re-tanning. The leather was processed on the lower floors of the buildings (Fig 45), where a copious supply of water was required for soaking and washing. Drying and sorting took

Fig 41 *John White's Rushden factory was built in a garden setting in 1938. White considered it to be the most beautiful factory in the shoe trade and was upset when the authorities removed the railings to help the war effort. The factory closed in the 1990s and has been converted into apartments. [BB97/05800]*

Fig 42 *R Griggs & Co's factory was built on the outskirts of Irthlingborough in 2000. It is in a modern hi-tech style, reflecting the image of the company's Dr Martens footwear. Although superior to the average out-of-town industrial unit, it is already redundant. It closed following the firm's announcement, in 2002, that it was moving all of its production to China, with the loss of more than 1,000 jobs. [AA026817]*

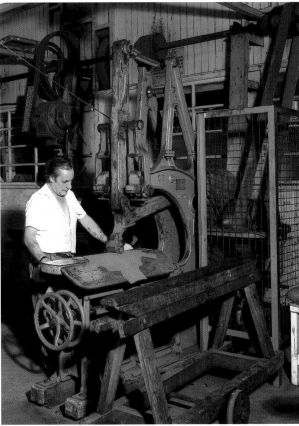

Figs 43 *and 44 W Pearce's tannery was designed by Wilfrid Lawson Carter and built in the years 1937–9 in spacious landscaped grounds at Billing Park, outside Northampton. These photographs show the stylish interior of the administration block lobby (with a view through to the production floor), and glazing machinery inside the factory. Although the building is listed, its future is uncertain. [BB018400; BB018411]*

Fig 45 *In 1899 the currying firm of Dickens Bros moved into a very simple four-storey factory, built by the local firm of A P Hawtin, on Kettering Road, Northampton. This photograph of 1929 illustrates the first floor of the factory.* [BB99/05290]

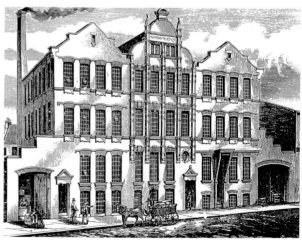

Fig 47 *The Jacobean-style Globe Leather Works was built at 4–6 Dunster Street, Northampton, for Collier's in 1887 and extended in 1889. The building is currently empty, but has planning permission for conversion to flats.* [From The Boot and Shoe Trades Journal, *Supplement, 7 March 1891; Northampton Museums and Art Gallery*]

Fig 46 *This former currier's, at 1 Dunster Street, Northampton, was built by G Heap for Collier's in 1877, and extended shortly afterwards. Despite hosting a variety of occupants during the 20th century, the building – now an upholstery works – retains many original features. (*See also *Fig 7.)*

place on the upper floors and in the attic space. Externally, the most distinctive features of drying lofts were wooden louvres or windows designed for maximum ventilation to assist the drying process. Louvres survive at Collier's (Fig 46) on Dunster Street, Northampton, where nails hammered neatly into the rafters, still with fragments of string attached, hint at how hides were hung for drying. Factories like this were outdated by the turn of the century: Collier's itself moved across the road into more spacious new premises – the Globe Leather Works (Fig 47) – in the late 1880s. By then, louvres were being abandoned in favour of uniform fenestration, as new drying techniques – using fan- or blast-drying chambers – were introduced. From the street, Collier's Globe Leather Works and other later leather-dressing factories closely resembled neighbouring shoe factories.

Wholesale leather merchants from all over the country opened establishments in Northampton. From impressive town-centre premises (Fig 48), equipped with offices and sample rooms, they sold leather to the commercial travellers or buyers who flocked to Northampton, as well as to local manufacturers. Several of these firms, such as Brice's, also had their own leather works.

## Other specialist buildings

Northamptonshire abounds in industrial buildings that owe their existence to the boot and shoe industry, but were not actually used to process leather or to manufacture footwear. In particular, a great deal of shoe machinery was made in the county. The oldest machinery works included Henry Mobbs's Lion Foundry and Vulcan Works in Northampton (Cow Lane and 34–8 Guildhall Road respectively), Owen Robinson's Champion Works in Kettering (Victoria Street) and Salmon & Co's Victoria Works, also in Kettering (Victoria Street). In 1888 the Northampton Shoe Machinery Co was founded by seven major manufacturers, first to market American lasting machines, then to manufacture them under licence. It erected new premises on Earl Street in 1888–9, comprising an office, showroom and machine store to the front, and a single-storey workshop to the rear. Later machinery works included the Arts and Crafts style Perfecta Works (Fig 49) on Catesby Street, Kettering, and the recently demolished Northampton Machinery Co Works (Fig 50) on Balfour Road, Northampton.

The most prominent commercial machinery warehouse in Northampton was Goodyear Chambers (Fig 51), a dignified building on the corner of Abington Street and Lower Mounts. Goodyear was one of three companies that amalgamated in 1899 to form the British United Shoe Machinery Company, which leased machinery – produced in the firm's works in Leicester – to manufacturers. The company erected several repair depots throughout Northamptonshire, including premises in Kettering (1910, School Lane), Rushden (c 1910, Midland Road) and Northampton (1923, Upper Mounts).

A number of firms specialised in the production of wooden lasts. These are foot-shaped forms, which could be made by turning lathes.

Fig 48 *The Northampton premises of the Glasgow-based leather merchants Malcolm Inglis & Co, designed by Alexander Ellis Anderson, are decorated with bulls' heads. This building at 50 Fish Street has recently been converted into apartments after a spell as a public house. Built in 1900, it stands opposite the firm's earlier warehouse, which was by the architects Mosley & Anderson. [AA044176]*

Fig 49 *(above, left) The deceptively domestic-looking Perfecta Works in Kettering was built in 1904 to a design by Timson, Bullock & Barber. A wide variety of boot and shoe machinery was manufactured in this building. [BB029378]*

Fig 50 *(above, right) The Northamptonshire Machinery Co Ltd factory on Balfour Road, Northampton, was designed by Sir John Brown & A E Henson and built in 1937. It has recently been demolished. Lt Gen Sir John Brown was articled to Charles Dorman in the 1890s and designed an innovative extension for Crockett & Jones (see Fig 38) with his first professional partner in 1910. [BB001827]*

Fig 51 *(right) Goodyear Chambers, Abington Street, is a landmark building in the centre of Northampton. It was built as a machinery warehouse in 1891, to designs by the local architect Edmund Law, and was extended in 1931 in a matching style. [BB013406]*

Once the components of shoes were made up, they were assembled over lasts to give them their shape. The last factory of O A Miller – an American manufacturer – was built on Arthur Street, Northampton, in 1896 and is now a shoe factory. Another important last manufacturer was Mobbs & Lewis. The firm's 'Easy-Exit' last, produced from 1885, prevented the back seam bursting when the last was extracted from the finished shoe. The Mobbs & Lewis factory (Fig 52) in Carrington Street, Kettering, was entirely rebuilt between 1961 and 1963, at a time when the company was switching from Canadian maple to plastic. One year later, in 1964, the O A Miller Last Co Ltd merged with Mobbs & Lewis to become Mobbs Miller. Another very important last works was R Whitton's, built at 21 St James's Road, Northampton, in 1932, and currently empty.

Fig 52 *The last works of Mobbs & Lewis (from 1964 Mobbs Miller) in Kettering was built in the years 1961–3, and was one of the largest post-war manufacturing plants serving the boot and shoe industry. It has now closed. [AA044209]*

Other factories, of all shapes and sizes, manufactured items such as grindery (the metal bits and pieces used in shoemaking, such as nails and eyelets), shoe laces, heels, sewing threads, stiffeners, dyes, polishes and cardboard boxes. Many of these businesses occupied converted shoe factories rather than purpose-built premises.

## Houses

Finally, housing forms a conspicuous element of boot and shoe communities, not just the terraced houses of the workers, but the houses of the factory owners and managers as well. The earliest factories, and those belonging to 'small masters', lay behind houses that occupied the street frontage. In later years, many boot and shoe factories were built in association with a house. While this usually stood alongside, or even behind, the factory, occasionally it was integrated to the point of invisibility (Fig 53).

Managers' houses (*see* Fig 36) are very modest, only slightly larger than neighbouring terraced houses. Owners' houses, on the other hand, were usually detached and double-fronted. Many were built close to factories, including Stephen Walker's substantial house of 1899, 'The Laurels', in Walgrave. By then, however, the most successful urban manufacturers were retreating to the suburbs, or even to country houses. In Northampton, some lived in the handsome villas in the Cliftonville and Billing Road area, while others built their own houses. In 1899, for example, Charles Dorman designed a neo-Jacobean-style mansion at Weston Favell for James Manfield; this later became Manfield Hospital. Manfield's brother Harry was among others who quit the noise and bustle of the town and moved to country estates.

Fig 53 *The boot and shoe factory at 83 High Street South, Rushden, was built in 1874. A two-storey house at the front of the building, served by a broad stack, is sandwiched between the basement and upper floor of the factory. This ingenious idea, prompted perhaps by the steeply sloping site, does not seem to have caught on. The entire building is now in residential use. [BB001997]*

# Conservation management and the future

by Ann Bond

As this book has demonstrated, the buildings associated with the Northampton boot and shoe industry are very varied and combine on the streets of the county's towns and villages to create a rich and harmonious environment. Now that we are in a position to understand and appreciate that landscape, we are better equipped to manage it for the future.

One of the most remarkable features of the Northamptonshire boot and shoe industry is that footwear is still being produced today in factories of the 19th and early 20th centuries, using traditional techniques, skills and, in some cases, machinery. A few firms still use their historic premises and continue to give us a fascinating picture of how the buildings work.

The story of the boot and shoe industry in Northamptonshire adds another dimension to our understanding of the Industrial Revolution. Late in developing into an industry, it never fully lost the craft beginnings that remain embodied in many small-scale workshops.

The surviving workshops and factories represent a rare legacy. It is one bequeathed by an industry that was dependent upon skilled workers, both outworkers and factory hands. The tradition of combining factory production with outworking and subcontracting, in a process that involved more than 200 distinct operations, led to the creation of extremely flexible workspaces that could be used in many different ways. These adaptable buildings are very characteristic of the industry.

Nationally, our industrial heritage can impress with buildings of awe-inspiring scale and processes involving immense power. In contrast, the buildings of the footwear industry are characterised by their modest functionality and the discreet way in which they are integrated into the urban texture. This is one of their greatest charms but, ironically, it is this very modesty and discretion that has, perhaps, caused them to be overlooked and undervalued.

Fig 54 *Henry Harday manufactured boots and shoes on Regent Street, Northampton, from at least 1850, making this one of the oldest surviving factory locations in the town. Now redundant, the building could still be successfully reused for a range of purposes, although most of its interior has been lost. [AA026822]*

We know that the surviving buildings represent only a small sample of the chronological, geographical and typological range that once existed. For example, there is little surviving evidence of buildings erected before 1870, and the currier's on Dunster Street (*see* Figs 7 and 46) and Miller's last works on Arthur Street, Northampton, are among the few remaining examples of once-common types.

Despite this patchy survival pattern, existing buildings give us a clear picture of an industry that had a relatively short, brilliant and hectic heyday between 1870 and 1920. At this time, a strong entrepreneurial spirit prevailed, resulting in energetic building activity. Sites developed in different ways. On some, a firm enjoyed gradual growth reflected in several phases of expansion, while on others a succession of different owners swiftly outgrew the premises and moved on. It is rare to find a factory or workshop that does not show the effects of one of these patterns of occupation, where change and continuity are closely linked. In conservation terms we have a tendency to ascribe the highest historic value to buildings that remain unaltered, but in this case the changes themselves are an interesting part of the story that the buildings have to tell.

The English Heritage survey, conducted between 1999 and 2001, identified more than 450 buildings (excluding garden workshops) associated with the boot and shoe industry in the county, with only 76 (17 per cent) still in footwear or leather trades use at that time. The pattern is not uniform, however. Rushden still retained 30 per cent of its boot and shoe buildings in related uses, while Wellingborough had only 7.5 per cent. Of the buildings surveyed, 21 per cent were vacant or undergoing redevelopment or demolition and 13 per cent had already undergone residential conversion. These figures are a snapshot in time and do not tell us about the rate of change. But judging from the number of planning applications (about 60) that have concerned these buildings since 2001, we can state with confidence that change is rapid.

Despite the fact that the industry has so dramatically contracted in Northamptonshire, the progressive abandonment of inconvenient, outmoded and surplus accommodation over a long period of time has not brought about the widespread dereliction that is characteristic of so

Fig 55 *A typical cast-iron window which says 'factory' to us all, lighting the first floor of the former Hawkins's factory on St Michael's Road, Northampton. One of the most effective ways of safeguarding the character of factory and workshop buildings is to retain these original windows. Note the low sill, the opening hopper and the hot-water heating pipes. [AA044156]*

many industrial landscapes. The local economy has remained sufficiently buoyant to prevent this from happening. There are, nevertheless, numerous vacant or partially used factories (Fig 54) in the county that are under threat from long-term lack of maintenance, radical conversion or, ultimately, demolition.

For many years, factories and large workshops created for the boot and shoe industry have been passing into other uses, with low-level occupation and under-used upper floors often leading to poor maintenance. Detached workshops are particularly vulnerable to conversion to garaging, and, as their materials start to reflect their age, general lack of maintenance and unsympathetic repair are common. Attached workshops are prone to integration into domestic accommodation or conversion into separate dwellings. Multi-storey factories are attractive for residential and office conversions. Single-storey factories are more difficult to adapt to non-industrial uses and few examples now survive with anything but their front office range. Both Manfield's on Wellingborough Road, Northampton (*see* Fig 40), and The Charles Parker Building, Midland Road, Higham Ferrers, once fronted extensive single-storey factory floors.

All forms of reuse can be beneficial, ensuring an active and useful future for buildings. However, a careful and sympathetic approach is needed if important characteristic features (Fig 55) and significant historic plan forms are to survive. In the best cases, external appearances are kept intact. This involves the retention of original or early doors and windows, taking-in doors (with their attendant winches, *see* Fig 53), distinctive plaques, datestones, roofing materials and rainwater goods. Sympathetic schemes will also take account of rear, ancillary or added ranges. These can be reused, but are frequently undervalued and are especially vulnerable to demolition to provide parking and amenity space. Schemes that retain the open expanses of former factory floors, with staircases, exposed brick walls and roof structures, timber floors and supporting cast-iron columns, really preserve the essence of the character of factory interiors, as seen in Figs 31–4. Attention to such details is the key to successful and appropriate conversions.

Fig 56 *The Britannia Slugging Machine Works, Oak Street, Rushden, demonstrates the vulnerability of boot and shoe buildings. It was built in 1899 as an engineering works producing riveting machinery for the footwear industry. It was constructed in a charming Italianate style with surprisingly elaborate detailing. Adapted to footwear production by Artisans Footwear Ltd, it remained in production until the 1990s. Despite its potential for reuse, it was demolished in 2002, and the site redeveloped for housing. [BB001748]*

The scale and urgency of the threat to these buildings and landscapes should not be underestimated (Fig 56). As a result of the survey, we are now in a much better position to appreciate and evaluate the importance of the surviving individual buildings of the Northamptonshire boot and shoe industry. There remains, however, considerable scope for enhancing our understanding of this industrial urban and rural landscape as a whole by analysing the historic character in a systematic way. This can be a major tool in the integration of important historic assets within an overall vision for social, economic and environmental revitalisation. By coming to a better understanding of what is important and why, we can encourage the positive management of change.

To achieve this there are two distinct processes within the legislative framework that can be followed: the listing of individual buildings and the designation of conservation areas.

Listed building legislation allows us to recognise, protect and regulate changes to individual buildings of 'special architectural or historic interest'. English Heritage advises central government which buildings are of special interest and they are designated by the Secretary of State. Those buildings and structures that are the best and most complete examples of the different building types associated with the boot and shoe industry, or are rare examples that survive in a relatively complete form, will be recommended for protection by being 'listed'. This is a very selective process, but in 2003–4 alone no less than twenty-four boot and shoe factories were added to the lists.

Through the designation of conservation areas, the planning system permits local authorities to identify, protect and manage change within 'areas of special architectural or historic interest which it is desirable to preserve and enhance'. As a result of the extensive survey and the mapping of the distribution of the surviving buildings, it is now possible to identify areas of urban landscape and industrialised villages where the industry has had a strong influence in shaping the character and sense of place. The designation of conservation areas is concerned with the preservation of the distinctive character of an area as a whole, rather than concentrating on individually selected buildings.

Both measures bring about significant changes to the way buildings and areas are managed:

- The special interest of a building or area is formally recognised.
- The building or area is legally protected.

In addition, Local Plans can provide a framework for sound conservation management within important historic areas. Local planning authorities are encouraged in government guidance to establish and maintain lists of locally important buildings. These do not have the legal protection afforded to listed buildings, but a building included in a 'Local List' does receive special consideration if there are plans for significant change. This form of designation would be particularly appropriate for the surviving buildings of the boot and shoe industry that are not otherwise protected by the two statutory means described above.

There is a growing recognition that the successful reuse of historic buildings can be a major factor in bringing about the regeneration of historic areas (Fig 57). As well as ensuring that the character of particular buildings and whole areas is not eroded, it can contribute in a positive way to a more sustainable future. Not only is it sensible to reuse buildings on account of the 'embodied energy' costs (the real costs of producing and transporting the materials of which they are made), but reuse that encourages the integration of home and work need not depend so heavily on environmentally damaging transport. This approach is particularly applicable to the former footwear-producing areas of Northamptonshire, where the relationship between factories, workshops and homes was always intimate.

Fortunately, most of the surviving buildings relating to the industry can be adapted to new uses, including retail, light industrial or office use (Fig 58). Given a sympathetic and flexible approach, most can have a continuing economic future and still retain their special interest, character and historic fabric. Today the greatest pressure is for housing. This often requires more extensive alterations, and consequently greater loss of character, than other uses. The key to revitalising such historic

Fig 57 *A combination of redevelopment and reuse has regenerated Duke Street in Northampton, which was home to Church's main factory until the late 1950s. This view, taken in December 2003, can be compared with the frontispiece image of this book, shot in 1999. The building in the foreground, an apartment block called the Lightbox (2001), occupies the site of Heggs's curriery, which was damaged by fire in 2000. [AA044240]*

Fig 58 *This building at 37 Regent St, Kettering (see Fig 15), exemplifies the successful reuse of a former factory as a retail unit, in this case a bedding showroom. This is an ideal 'loose-fit' solution, requiring few internal or external alterations. The factory, with its attractive original windows, still forms an integral part of a characteristic urban street scene: industrial and domestic buildings sit together in harmony, creating an unbroken line, extending right up to the pavement. Scenes such as this, which encapsulate the unique character of the Northamptonshire boot and shoe industry, can be protected by selectively designating conservation areas. [AA044169]*

buildings and areas is to aim for a degree of mixed use, reflecting the historic pattern of diversity. This can bring about the vitality that exclusive residential use seldom achieves.

Conservation is not only about buildings. It is about people's history, their sense of place, and the quality of life that this confers. The neighbourhood industrial buildings have been a part of the lives of local people for a very long time, defining the everyday scene and often inspiring considerable pride. The buildings that survive today are inextricably linked with a particular way of life and community identity. Most of us would agree that they should be vital, viable places that retain their distinguishing characteristics. If we can achieve this, we will have preserved the best of the past for the future. This is the challenge before us.

# Listed buildings relating to the boot and shoe industry in Northamptonshire
## (All buildings are listed grade II.)

### Desborough
Joseph Cheaney & Sons, Rushton Road and Regent Street

### Kettering
Dalkeith Works, Green Lane
Factory (now Bathcraft), off Havelock Street
Globe Works, Bath Road and Digby Street
Ken Hall Footwear (formerly Newman & Sons), Newman Street
Regent Works (now Kettering Bedding Centre), 37 Regent Street

### Long Buckby
Outworkers' Workshops, behind 45–53 East Street

### Northampton
Collier's (currier's, now A J Tear & Co), 1 Dunster Street
Crockett & Jones, Perry Street, Magee Street and Turner Street
Enterprise Factory (formerly A Lee, now Expert Developments), Bective Road
Factory, 3 Gray Street
Footshape Boot Works (formerly William Barratt & Co), Kingsthorpe Road
G T Hawkins (formerly part Hornby & West, part G T Hawkins), Overstone Road and Dunster Street
Globe Leather Works (formerly Collier's), 4–6 Dunster Street

Malcolm Inglis & Co (leather warehouse), 50 Fish Street
Mobbs Miller House (formerly CWS), listed with front walls, railings and gates, Christchurch Road
Monks Park Factory (formerly M P Manfield & Sons), 369 Wellingborough Road
O A Miller Last Works (now Rushton Ablett and Park Lane Windows), Arthur Street and Bunting Road
Speedwell Works (now J L & Co), Oliver Street
Tricker's, 54–60 St Michael's Road
Unicorn Works, 20–6 St Michael's Road
Vulcan Works (formerly H Mobbs), 34–8 Guildhall Road
W Pearce (tannery), Billing Park
Workshops and houses, 41 and 43 Colwyn Road

### Raunds
Ernest Chambers Heel Factory (now Wescam Engineering), Park Road

### Rushden
Cromwell Works (William Green & Sons), Upper Queen Street
Cunnington Brothers, Crabb Street
Factory, 5a and 7 Crabb Street
John White (Impregnable Boots), Higham Road

### Wollaston
Workshops, behind 28–38 London Road

# Walking tour of Northampton's core boot and shoe district
## (*see* map on inside back cover)

The following key identifies some of the most interesting boot and shoe buildings in Northampton. Many others can be seen scattered throughout this area to the north-east of the town centre, and in other parts of town. Take in sites 1 to 13 for a short walk of one to one-and-a-half hours; to see every site will take approximately three hours.

1   19–20 Guildhall Road. Originally a leather warehouse (1876, with later extensions), once occupied by Phipps and now Derngate Theatre. On the other side of the road, the Northampton Museum and Art Gallery houses a boot and shoe collection of national importance. Henry Mobbs's Vulcan Works of 1877 is at No. 34.

2   50 Fish Street. Built for Malcolm Inglis & Co, leather merchants, in 1900. (*See* Fig 48.)

3   63 Abington Street. Built for W C Henderson, leather merchant, in 1897.

4   85 Abington Street. Goodyear Chambers, built for the Goodyear Shoe Machinery Company (later the British United Shoe Machinery Company) in 1891, and extended in 1931. Now BBC Radio Northampton. (*See* Fig 51.)

5   Junction of Overstone Road and St Michael's Road. Two footwear factories: Hornby & West's of 1876 (extended 1883 and 1893) and G T Hawkins's of 1886 (extended 1888, 1893 and 1914). (*See* Figs 7, 26, 29, 37 and 55.)

6   1 Dunster Street. Currier's built for Collier's in 1877. (*See* Figs 7 and 46.)

7   4–6 Dunster Street. The Globe Leather Works, built for Collier's in the years 1887–9. (*See* Figs 7 and 47.)

8   56–64 Dunster Street. Erected in the 1890s, this range of single-storey buildings – probably leather warehouses – housed a variety of leather trades. To reach St Michael's Road use the alley beside No. 84 (note workshop to rear).

9   105 St Michael's Road. A boot and shoe factory, occupied by H J Bateman in the late 19th century.

10  Behind 69 Kettering Road. Leather works built in 1899 by Dickens Bros, and still occupied by the same firm. (*See* Fig 45.)

11  62 St Michael's Road. A boot and shoe factory of 1883, once occupied by Pollard & Son.

12  54–60 St Michael's Road. R E Tricker's boot and shoe factory, with façade of 1924. (*See* Fig 39.)

13  22–6 St Michael's Road. A pair of factories, speculatively built about 1885; for much of its existence Beale & Co's Unicorn Works.

14  25–9 Robert Street. Built as a currier's in the late 1880s and occupied by W H Heggs throughout most of its history. There are a number of other factories on Robert Street and nearby Connaught Street.

15  19 Thomas Street (now Mounts Business Centre). Built as a shoe factory in the early 1890s and occupied for short time by Padmore & Barnes.

16  20 Bailiff Street. House with rear workshop on Robert Street, probably built about 1870. (*See* Fig 21.)

17  Duke Street. Church's former factory was built in 1877 and was extended in 1893. (*See* Frontispiece and Fig 57.) Walking west along Louise Road and Lorne Road several other small factories of the 1870s and 1880s can be seen.

18  3 Gray Street. Factory of about 1890, occupied by a succession of different manufacturers, including shoe mercers.

19  1 Colwyn Road. A boot and shoe factory of the late 1880s, occupied by James Birch, and later by W F Strickland.

20  41–3 Colwyn Road. Two houses with rear workshops built in the late 1880s. Stand in park for best view.

21  17–19 Hood Street. The Accurate Boot Works, probably built in the late 1880s.

22  20 Shakespeare Road/75–6 Cowper Street. Built as a boot and shoe factory (Cowper Factory) for Henry Sharman about 1886. Note the 'Lennards Ltd' painted sign on the façade.

23  Grove Road/Clare Street. G M Tebbutt's Grove Works, built in 1889. (*See* Fig 33.)

24  15 Turner Street. A boot and shoe factory of the late 1880s, occupied by a succession of different manufacturers.

25  Perry Street/Magee Street/Turner Street. The boot and shoe factory of Crockett & Jones, built in 1889–90 and extended in 1896, 1910 and 1935. (*See* Figs 6 and 38.)

26  Adnitt Road/Stimpson Avenue. Additions of 1913 and 1925 (now façade only) to the boot and shoe factory of J Sears & Co (True-Form).

27  Artizan Road/Henry Street. A pair of boot and shoe factories of 1893, used by J T Meadows & Sons as a leather works from 1911. A number of other factories can be seen on Henry Street.

28  9–12 Palmerston Road (Palmerston House). An 1870s boot and shoe factory, occupied by A Jones & Sons in the mid-20th century. (*See* Fig 28.)

29  66 Palmerston Road. Boot and shoe factory built in the late 1880s for John & Joseph Brown and occupied by A Jones & Sons between 1911 and 1955, then by Church's between 1955 and 1966.

30  Off Woodford Street. Factory and workshop, probably built in the 1880s and occupied by various boot and shoe manufacturers.

31  12 Ethel Street (The Works). Built in 1875 and occupied by a succession of boot and shoe manufacturers.

32  Between 42 and 44 Victoria Road. Built in 1873 as a boot and shoe factory.

33  32–4 Victoria Road. Built about 1880 and occupied by a succession of boot and shoe manufacturers.

34  10–12 Victoria Road. Built in the mid-1870s for the boot and shoe manufacturer G Webb.

35  2 Victoria Road. Built in the mid-1870s for the boot and shoe manufacturer James Walding.

# Acknowledgements

This book is largely based on a survey carried out by Adam Menuge, Andrew Williams, Kathryn Hilsden and Jonathan Cooke. The graphics were produced by Allan T Adams; the photographs were taken by Pat Payne and the aerial photographs were taken by Damian Grady.

We would like to acknowledge the assistance of the following individuals: Jennifer Ballinger (of Northamptonshire County Council), Dr Garry Campion, Colin Clayson, Sue Constable (of Northampton Museum), Martin Ellison (formerly of Northamptonshire County Council, now of Kettering Borough Council), Peter Neaverson, Dr Marilyn Palmer, Geoffrey Starmer, June Swann and Dr Barrie Trinder. We would like to thank all the local firms and householders who generously gave us access to their properties and supplied historical information.

Front cover *The town of Northampton takes great pride in its long association with the boot and shoe trade. This Victorian capital in the porch of the Guildhall (E Godwin, 1861–4) shows an open-fronted medieval shoe shop attended by a shoemaker. [AA044243]*

Inside front cover *Closed uppers, ready for the making process (sole attachment), stored in Tricker's factory, St Michael's Road, Northampton. This well-known firm was established in London in 1829 and opened a factory in Northampton in 1903. [AA99/06682]*

Inside back cover *Map of Northampton's core boot and shoe district.*

Back cover *A relief of a Native American on the doorway of Church's current factory, St James's Road, Northampton. This factory, built in the late 1890s, was originally the Moccasin Works of Padmore & Barnes. [AA044149]*